My Cat Knows Karate

Funny Poems For Kids

Kenn Nesbitt
Illustrations By Rafael Domingos

16

EasyRead Large

RHYW

Copyright Page from the Original Book

TABLE OF CONTENTS

For Trey

My Cat Knows Karate

My cat knows karate.
My frog knows kung fu.
My poodle knows judo.
My turtle does too.

They all became black belts
by watching TV;
some Chuck Norris movies,
and films with Bruce Lee.

They liked learning lessons

from Jean-Claude Van Damme,
and acting like action-film star
Jackie Chan.

They practiced their punches,
their blocks, and their kicks
until they were masters
of martial arts tricks.

You'd think they'd be good now
at guarding our house,
but, yesterday morning,
they ran from my mouse.

My mouse is a crack-up.
I laughed at his prank.
Do you think it's weird that
my mouse drives a tank?

My Brother Ate My Smartphone

My brother ate my smartphone.
Although it might sound strange,
he swallowed it and, bit by bit,
his brains began to change.

He started getting smarter.
He grew so shrewd and wise.
And I could see that, suddenly,
a light was in his eyes.

He knew as much as Google.

His IQ was off the charts.
I'd never seen someone so keen,
with such astounding smarts.

He solved the toughest problems
with simplicity and ease,
and calculated answers
with unrivaled expertise.

It seems he's now a genius;
a perfect Brainiac.
But I don't care, or think it's fair.
I want my smartphone back.

Olympic Granny

When Grandma goes for gold in
the Olympic games this year,
she'll laugh at her competitors
and make them quake with fear.

She's ninety-nine years old
but, in athletics, she's been
blessed.
The trouble is she can't decide
which sport she plays the best.

She's such an ace at archery.
She's queen of the canoe.
She's tough to top at taekwondo
and table tennis too.

She dominates the diving board.
She tromps the trampoline.
At lifting weights and wrestling
she's the best you've ever seen.

She speeds across the swimming
pool
to slake the summer heat.
On BMX and mountain bike
she simply can't be beat.

She's highest in the high jump,
and a champ at hammer throwing,
magnificent in marathons,
remarkable at rowing.

She beats the best at boxing.
At the pole vault she is peerless.
Her fencing is the finest;
she is positively fearless.

She's masterful at basketball,
(she truly rules the court),
and equally incredible
at every other sport.

But what we find astonishing
and something of a shocker
is how she wins all contests
with her wheelchair and her walker.

My Virtual Puppy

I purchased a virtual puppy.
He lives in an app on my phone.
He digs in a virtual garden
to bury a virtual bone.

I feed him with virtual dog food.
I'm teaching him virtual tricks,
like giving me virtual handshakes
and fetching his virtual sticks.

He naps on a virtual sofa.

He likes to chase virtual cats.
Whenever he's good I reward him
with virtual dog treats and pats.

He'll bring me the virtual paper.
He'll chew on a virtual shoe.
There's only one virtual problem.
I clean up his virtual poo.

Joe the Emoji

I'm Joe the Emoji.
I 😁 when I'm glad.
I 😠 when I'm angry.
I 🙁 when I'm sad.
Whenever I'm silly
my 😜 goes like this.
I 😉 if I like you,
or blow you a 😘.
I 😴 when I'm tired.
I 😭 when afraid.
I have the most flexible
😐 ever made.

I hope that you 👍 me
and don't think I'm rude.
I'm Joe the Emoji.
I'm one 😎 dude.

Pimple Problem

I had a little problem.
It gave me quite a scare.
I looked into the mirror
and saw a pimple there.

That pimple was enormous
and growing on my nose,
both bigger than a button,
and redder than a rose.

I knew my friends would notice.

I thought that they would stare.
I figured they would laugh at me
to see that pimple there.

So that's when I decided
to give them a surprise.
I grabbed a pen and drew on it
two tiny little eyes.

I drew a nose, a mouth, two ears,
a mustache, and a beard,
to make my pimple obvious
and wonderful and weird.

My drawing was a winner
and a hit with every friend.
Now painting on our pimples
is the hottest fashion trend.

Our Teacher Likes Minecraft

Our teacher likes Minecraft.
She plays it all day.
She tells us to study
so she can go play.

She'll dig in her mine,
going deeper and deeper,
then fight off a skeleton,
zombie, or creeper.

She'll engineer buildings
from dirt, wood, and stone,
then go out exploring
the landscape alone.

She'll build and collect and
she'll run, jump, and swing.
There's only one problem...
we don't learn a thing.

I Miss My Sister

I miss my sister all the time.
For her it's not the same.
She never misses me at all.
She has a better aim.

November Is upon Us

November is upon us.
Thanksgiving's nearly here.
I've never been more thankful than
the way I feel this year.

I'm thankful we have apple pie.
I'm thankful we have beans.
I'm thankful we have mashed
potatoes,
yams, and salad greens.

But, most of all, I'm thankful that
my future isn't murky.
My family's vegetarian
and I am their pet turkey.

Wendy Wise

There was a girl named Wendy
Wise,
who didn't like to exercise.
She wouldn't ever lift a weight,
or skip a rope, or roller skate.
You'd never see her ride a bike,
or bounce a ball, or take a hike.
She wouldn't run, or trot, or jog,
or go outside and walk the dog.
She wouldn't skip or climb a hill,
or practice any kind of skill
like jumping rope or playing ball.
She wouldn't exercise at all.

It's no surprise that Wendy Wise,
who didn't like to exercise,
would pass away one fateful day,
and in a rather tragic way.
You see, that morning, in the sky,
a tiny bird was flying by.
It lost a feather, small and brown,
that slowly, slowly, drifted down.
It landed right on Wendy's head
and knocked her down and killed
her dead.
She was, it seems, so frail and
weak,
with such a sickly, sad physique
that, when that feather touched
her hair,
it did her in, right then and there.

Poor Wendy! What an awful shame.
If only she had played a game,
or went outside to run around,
or practiced jumping up and down,
or had a swim, or took a dive,
today she might still be alive.

Regrettably, it's now too late,
and Wendy Wise has met her fate.
But I, my friend, would much
prefer

that you do not end up like her.
So please go out and play a game,
because, you see, despite her
name,
to never, ever exercise,
like Wendy, isn't very wise.

The Games in My Room

The video games that
I keep in my room,
like Tetris, Terraria,
Minecraft, and Doom,
and one about somebody
raiding a tomb,
and one with invaders from
space...

They're up on the dresser
and down on the floor.
The Legend of Zelda
and Street Fighter IV,
and Roblox, and Pac Man,
and Fortnite, and more,
are scattered all over the place.

There's Sonic the Hedgehog
and Dragon Ball Z,
and Mario Party,
and Madden for Wii,
and FIFA 18 for the
Playstation 3.

They're littered and strewn all
around.

There's Kidz Sports and Kirby
and Kingdom Hearts II,
Jurassic Park, Jeopardy,
Just Dance Wii U,
and don't forget Pokémon
Red, Green, and Blue,
all over the bed and the ground.

They're under my bed
in a battered old box.
They're tossed in the closet
with Legos and blocks.
They're stuffed in a drawer
with my undies and socks.
They're thrown around every which
way.

It's kind a problem.
It's sort of a shame.
It's clearly my fault.
No one else is to blame.
The game I can't locate
is always the same...
it's the one that I'm wanting to
play.

I Rode a Rainbow Unicorn

I rode a rainbow unicorn.
We sailed across the sky.
(I'd fed him lots of Skittles,
since they always make him fly.)

We took off like a comet
on a long and graceful flight.
And everywhere the people stopped
and marveled at the sight.

His path was bright and colorful.
It sparkled, shimmered, shined,
as he arced across the heavens
shooting rainbows from behind.

The Cough

There was a man who coughed a cough,
a cough so strong his head fell off.
His head fell off. It hit the ground.
It hit the ground and rolled around.
It rolled around and rolled away,
away into a field of hay,
a field of hay that caused a wheeze,
a wheeze that turned into a sneeze,
a sneeze he sneezed from dusk till dawn.

At dawn he sneezed his head back
on.

Five-Sense Nonsense

I saw a saw.
I felt some felt.
I heard a herd.
I smelt a smelt.
I ate at eight.
So tell me, do,
does this make any
sense to you?

Glurp the Purple Alien

I'm Glurp, the purple alien.
I come from outer space.
I have a purple body.
I have a purple face.
I use my purple tentacles
to dine on purple food.
The treats I find the tastiest
are purely purple-hued.

I'll eat a purple burger.
I'll slurp a purple shake.
I'll feast on purple pickles

and partake of purple cake.
I'll nosh on purple noodles.
I'll feast on purple fries.
I'll munch on purple macaroons
and purple pizza pies.
I haven't seen your planet,
but, if I ever do,
you'd better not wear purple;
I might just dine on you.

I Fix My Duck with Duct Tape

I fix my duck with duct tape
when she breaks. That's what I do.
If my gorilla has a crack
I use Gorilla Glue.

My monkey needs a monkey
wrench
just every now and then.
And chicken wire is what I use
to mend my broken hen.

For snails, I use nails,

and, for penguins, I use pins.
For fish, I'm fond of fish paste
for fixing fractured fins.

So bring your broken beasts;
I'll give them tender loving care,
and make them good as new at my
stuffed animal repair.

When Chemists Die, They Barium

When chemists die, they barium.
Dead kings get throne away.
Magicians simply disappear.
Dog catchers go astray.

When chauffeurs pass, they lose
their drive.
Dead ranchers get deranged.
Composers simply decompose,
while bankers are unchanged.

It's said that swimmers have a
stroke.
Mechanics are retired.
The end for human cannonballs
is often when they're fired.

Librarians, they just check out.
Shoemakers get the boot.
Old cows just kick the bucket, and
dead owls don't give a hoot.

When travel agents go
they take a permanent vacation,

and dead cartoonists end up
in suspended animation.

Santa Brought a Bar of Soap

Santa brought a bar of soap.
I asked him for a phone, but nope.
I didn't get that brand new phone;
just soap, and fancy French
cologne.
He also brought some new
shampoo,
some shower gel, and toothpaste
too,
a scented candle for my room,
a dozen bottles of perfume,
deodorant and body spray...
I wonder what he's trying to say?

Josh the Sausage Maker

I'm Josh. I make sausage,
and roast beef and ham,
baloney and bacon,
and turkey and Spam.

I also make meatloaf,
pancetta, pastrami,
prosciutto and hot dogs,
corned beef and salami.

But liverwurst sausage
is what I do best,
and everyone likes it
much more than the rest.

If anyone asks you,
you heard it here first.
I'm Josh. I make sausage.
My best is the wurst.

Pete the Pirate Wannabe

He's Pete, the pirate wannabe.
He'll sail the seas someday.
But, first, he needs a little cash
to help him on his way.

He can't afford a parrot.
He can't afford a plank.
A peg leg's much too pricey,
and ship would break the bank.

He cannot buy an eye patch.
He hasn't got a hat.
He'll never own a blunderbuss;
he's much too broke for that.

A dagger's too expensive.
He couldn't swing a sword.
In fact, there's only one thing
he's been able to afford.

His shopping list is lengthy,
with loads of pirate gear,
but all he has are earrings
since they're just a buck an ear.

Our Teacher's Not a Zombie

Our teacher's not a zombie.
She's not the living dead,
although she's looking ragged
and her eyes are rather red.

She shuffles to the classroom.

She slowly drags her feet.
She shambles to the whiteboard
looking broken-down and beat.

We listen to her plaintive moans.
We see the way she strains.
We hear her mumble mournfully
about the students' brains.

But we know not to worry.
We never get upset.
She's always like this when she
hasn't had her coffee yet.

Minecraft Mike

Hello, my friends. My name is Mike.
I never hike or ride a bike.
You see, the only thing I like
is playing lots of Minecraft.

I never run, or climb a tree,
or sail a ship across the sea.
Why, I don't even watch TV.
I just play lots of Minecraft.

I don't play sports of any sorts,
on basketball or tennis courts,
in training shoes or running shorts.
I'm only good at Minecraft.

You'll never see me pet the cat,
or shop online to buy a hat,
or instant message, text, or chat.
I'm busy playing Minecraft.

In fact, I'm busy as can be,
so if you'd like to talk to me,
there's just one way, and that, you see,
is multiplayer Minecraft.

1 H0P3 7H47 Y0U C4N R34D 7H15

1 H0P3 7H47 Y0U C4N R34D 7H15.
1'M PR377Y 5UR3 Y0U C4N.
17'5 7R1CKY, 4ND 1'M
W0ND3R1NG
1F Y0U W1LL UND3R574ND.

1 KN0W 7H47 17'5 4 PUZZL3.

1 KN0W 17'5 K1ND 0F 70UGH.
1 H0P3 7H47 Y0U D0N'7 734R 17 UP
4ND 5CR34M, "1'V3 H4D 3N0UGH!"

1'M 7YP1NG 7H15 7H3 0NLY W4Y
7H47 1 KN0W H0W 70D4Y.
1 H0P3 7H47 Y0U C4N F1GUR3 0U7
7H3 W0RD5 1'M 7RY1NG 70 54Y.

1F Y0U C4N R34D 7H15 M3554G3,
17 M34N5 Y0U'R3 R34LLY 5M4R7.
17 4L50 M34N5 7H47 MY
C0MPU73R'S K3YB04RD F3LL
4P4RT.

Perfect Parker Paul

There's no one whose as punctual
as Perfect Parker Paul.
He's never been a second late
for anything at all.

He owns eleven watches
that he wears upon his arms,
plus twenty seven cuckoo clocks
and forty nine alarms.

He wakes up extra early
to ensure he's never late.
He sets his clock for half-past-three
to get to school by eight.

You'll often find him in his room
just staring at his clocks.
Plus, everywhere that Parker goes
he runs instead of walks.

And when he gives a birthday gift
it's guaranteed to chime.
For Parker Paul there simply is
no present like the time.

To B or Not to B

I bought a black banana,
and a broken baseball bat.
A burst balloon, a busted boat,
a beat-up bowler hat.

I wasn't being brainy, bright,
or brilliant but, you see,
my brain was boggled after
being bitten by a bee.

Opposite Day

It's Opposite Day!
It's Opposite Day!
The day to do things
in the opposite way.

I wear my pants backward.
My shirt's inside out.
I scream to talk softly.
I whisper to shout.

I write with my foot and

I kick with my hand.
I stare with my eyes closed.
I sit down to stand.

I drink from a plate and
I eat from a cup.
I climb into bed when
it's time to wake up.

I frown when I'm happy.
I smile when I'm sad.
I say I like liver,
but ice cream is bad.

I claim that it's dark
when it's sunny and bright.
If something is black,
I insist that it's white.

I stand still for dancing.
When running, I crawl.
So please understand:
I don't like you at all.

I Tried to Take a Selfie

I tried to take a selfie
when I was all alone.
I never should have done it.
It broke my mobile phone.

I guess I'm not so pretty.
I thought that I was cuter.
I snapped one with my laptop
and busted my computer.

I cracked my father's camera.
My mother's iPad too.
This shouldn't be so difficult.
I don't know what to do.

At last I got a selfie;
perhaps the worst one yet.
I posted it online today.
It broke the Internet.

Love Sick

I'm feeling sick.
My face is red.
I'm dazed and dizzy
in my head.
I think I need to
stay in bed
at least about a week.

My stomach's tied
in awful knots.
I'm breaking out

with purple spots.
I'm seeing stars
and lots of dots.
I feel like I should shriek.

I don't know what
to do or say.
I'd never ever
felt this way,
until today
when Anna-Kay
kissed me on the cheek.

I Can't Get Enough of this Pokémon Go

I can't get enough of this Pokémon
Go.
The fever is on me
and starting to grow.
This game is amazing!
I thought you should know.
There's nothing I want to do more.

I play on the playground.
I play in the park.
I play in the daytime.
I play after dark.

I'm constantly playing,
but I should remark
this game sure is making me sore.

While playing today
I ran into a wall.
I stumbled and fell down
the stairs at the mall.
I tripped on the street and
had such a bad fall,
I probably fractured my toe.

My forehead is hurting.
My bottom feels bad.
This tripping and falling
is making me mad.
The game is amazing,
but maybe I've had
enough of this Pokémon Go.

Not-So-Fast Food

Burgers, pizzas, chicken wings.
Tacos, French fries, onion rings.
Ice cream, donuts, cookies, cakes.
Soda, chips, and chocolate shakes.
These are things I like to munch,
breakfast, dinner, snack, and lunch.

Every meal I eat includes
more, and more, and more fast
foods.
Yet with every meal I eat
I grow slower on my feet.
This is why I want to know
why does *fast* food make me *slow?*

My Sheep Is Being Sheepish

My sheep is being sheepish.
My cat is acting catty.
My horse, of course, is sort of
hoarse.
My bat's completely batty.

My chicken's plainly chicken.
My hare is fairly hairy.
My cuckoo's truly cuckoo.
My mare is very merry.

My fish is frankly fishy,
and so my flea is fleeing.
My slug is somewhat sluggish.
My bee is simply being.

I have so many animals
and this is how they're feeling,
except for one, who's tons of fun:
My seal is on the ceiling.

I Went to the Gym

I went the the gym.
I lifted a weight.
My muscles got bigger.
It felt really great.

I hoisted another,
a heavier one.
I got even stronger.
I thought it was fun.

I wandered outside where
I bent a steel bar.
I pulled up a park bench
and carried a car.
I picked up a truck
and then set out to try
to boost a big building
I'd spotted nearby.
So now I'm in jail with
my muscles to thank.
I probably shouldn't have
held up that bank.

A Sad and Lonely Cyclops

I'm a sad and lonely Cyclops.
I am so misunderstood.
Though I probably look fearsome
I am actually good.

I'm as harmless as a kitten.
No, I wouldn't hurt a fly,
But my neighbors think I'm
monstrous
with my solitary eye.

So they laugh at me and tease me
and they often call me names,
plus they won't let me participate
in their Olympic games.

They won't let me join their
practices
or even watch a tryout.
So I sit at home and sniffle
and I sadly cry my eye out.

Carl the Cookie Carrier

I'm Carl the Cookie Carrier.
I carry cookies well.
I carry ones with chocolate chips
and ones with caramel.

I transport tea cakes tactfully.
With wafers I'm an ace.
My gift for lifting biscuits
is the ultimate in grace.

I'm skilled with Scottish shortbread.
With digestives I'm the best.
With gingersnaps I have no lapse.
It's obvious I'm blessed.

I'm masterful with macaroons
and snickerdoodles too.
I'll haul them all regardless
if they're pink or green or blue.

And when I carry cookies,
I just eat one or two.
And so, there's just one question...
May I carry yours for you?

Inside Our Fridge

Inside our fridge there's still a smidge
of old and moldy ham.
And, next to it, there's just a bit
of dried-up, fried-up Spam.

The bacon in the crisper bin
has been there much too long.
The sausage links have such a stink;

their smell is simply wrong.

The ribs and roast are both the most
disgusting ever seen.
Yes, every piece has rancid grease
and spots of bluish-green.

We left it there without a care
for weeks, or months, or years.
Now all this rotten food we've got
is bringing us to tears.

I guess we should have understood
it must be eaten quick,
and if we wait till it's too late,
it might just make us sick.

But now this meat – too old to eat,
too fossilized to fork,
from long before the dinosaurs–
is all Jurassic Pork.

My Puppy Plays Piano

My puppy plays piano.
It's the strangest thing to see.
It seems, while I was practicing,
he learned by watching me.

He started out with chopsticks,

then he learned to play some
Bach.
It wasn't long before he knew
the blues and classic rock.

He also taught my kitten how
so they could play duets.
And then they taught guitar and
drums
to all my other pets.

They formed a band and practiced
hard
and traveled all around,
and instantly got famous
for their catchy "Pet Rock" sound.

They made a smash hit record
and it wasn't very long
before my pets were millionaires
because they wrote *this* song.

Hello, My Name Is Madison

Hello, my name is Madison.
I live on Lincoln Street.
I'm in the state of Washington.
I think that's pretty neat.

My middle name is Kennedy.
My last name is Monroe.

My name has got more Presidents
than anyone I know.

My father's name is Harrison.
My brother's name is Grant.
My mother's name is Reagan,
and Taylor is my aunt.

I go to Eisenhower School.
My family drives a Ford.
That's way too many Presidents
to ever be ignored.

It can't just be coincidence.
It's not some chance event.
When I grow up, it's obvious...
I'll be the President!

My Frog Recycles All His Trash

My frog recycles all his trash.
He eats organic food.
He cares for the environment.
He's quite the hipster dude.

Reduce, reuse, recycle
is the motto of my frog.
He drives a solar-powered car

to cut back on the smog.

He helps endangered species and
opposes climate change.
He knows that, since he's just a
frog,
this might seem kind of strange.

But, still, he does his very best
to keep our planet clean.
He thinks it's only natural.
He's proud of being green.

The Setter Sweater Store

My setter has a sweater
from The Setter Sweater Store.
It's better than the sweater
that my setter had before.

Her sweater has a letter
in the center of the chest.
(For the lettered setter sweaters
are what setters like the best.)

And if you ever met her
you could get to pet her sweater.
(You should pet a lettered sweater;
there's no setter sweater better!)

So if your pet's a setter
then I bet you'll pet her more
if you get her lettered sweaters
from The Setter Sweater Store.

A Shark Is a Pet

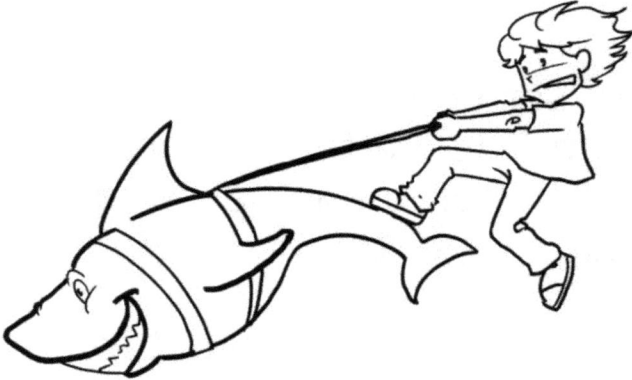

A shark is a pet
that you don't want to get.
There is nothing less fun than a
shark.
He doesn't have fur.
He won't cuddle or purr,
and he never takes walks in the
park.

Instead he just stares
and intensely prepares,
as he circles and waits in the dark,
to nibble your nose
and your fingers and toes
for his bite is much worse than his
bark.

I Had a Little Secret

I had a little secret
and I told a friend of mine.
I made her promise not to tell.
I thought it would be fine.

But then she told somebody else,
and they told someone too.
Then each of them told others,
and it grew, and grew, and grew.

Then someone posted it online.
It blossomed like a spiral.
The next thing that I knew,
my secret went completely viral.

It made the rounds on Instagram,

YouTube, and Twitter too.
It wasn't very long at all
till everybody knew.

So now my secret's everywhere
for all the world to see.
I'm guessing that's the last one
that you'll ever share with me.

Emilio, Emilio

Emilio, Emilio,
was never one to stealio,
but had no meat
or bread to eat;
not even an apple peelio.

Emilio, Emilio,
he got his rod and reelio,
to catch some fish
to fill his dish,
but all he caught were eelio.

Emilio, Emilio,
did not like eating eelio.
He sold them to
a merchant who
gave him an awesome dealio.

Emilio, Emilio,
at last I can revealio,
bought lots of meat
and bread to eat,
and a fancy new automobilio.

My Hat Is Full of Rabbits

My hat is full of rabbits.
My cape is full of doves.
A playing card is up my sleeve,
and more are in my gloves.

A wand is in my pocket
with handkerchiefs and flowers.
My coat has things like ropes and
rings
with mystifying powers.

I have my staff and juggling clubs,
my mirrors, cups, and dice,
my crystal ball, my smoke
machine,
and fancy dancing mice.

I'm ready for my magic show.
There's just one problem here...
My elephant is on my lap
and will not disappear.

Boney Mahoney

I'm Boney Mahoney,
the Skeleton Singer.
I'm known for harmonious tones.
I'll croon to the tune of
a jaw harp or hand drum.
I'll trill to the sound of trombones.

To have me start humming
just tickle the ivories.
I'll sing if you finger a bell.
I'll rap if you slap at
a washboard or rattle.

I'm hip to the nose flute as well.

If you're a musician
in search of a singer,
give Boney Mahoney a call.
But find someone else if
you only play organ;
I sing with no organs at all.

Cinderella, Soccer Player

Cinderella stunk at soccer.
She was bad at basketball.
Though equipment filled her locker
she could hardly play at all.

Baseball, football, hockey, tennis;
none were Cinderella's sport.
No one feared her speed or menace
on the field or rink or court.

Though she spent her evenings training,
and on weekends she would drill,
practicing without complaining,
she could not improve her skill.

Her performance wasn't stellar.
Still, she was beyond reproach.
That's because poor Cinderella
had a pumpkin for a coach.

I Made a New Password

I made a new password
That no one could guess.
It's long and confusing
And truly a mess.

It has random letters
and numbers galore,
with dozens of symbols
and spaces and more.

My password is perfect,
completely secure,
and no one will break it;
of that I am sure.

It's flawless and foolproof.
I don't have a doubt.
But, whoops! I forgot it
and now I'm locked out.

My Hare Is Resting on My Head

My hare is resting on my head.
I also have bear feet.
A swallow's in my throat
and there are calves below my
seat.

A seal is on my lips today.
A slug is on my fist.
A mussel's on my shoulder
and a tick is on my wrist.

A wasp is on my yellow jacket
where it likes to bee.
A fly is on my zipper,
though I wish that it would flea.

My doe is in my wallet
and my sole is on my shoe.
I hope my tail was not a boar.
What's gnu, my deer, with ewe?

My Puppy Ate My Earbuds

My puppy ate my earbuds.
My puppy ate my socks.
My puppy chewed my tennis shoes
and all my Lego blocks.

He gnawed upon my iPod
as if it were a bone.
He nibbled my Nintendo Switch
and munched my mobile phone.

He grazed upon my skateboard,

consumed my catcher's mitts,
and chomped my chess and
checkers sets
to tiny little bits.

He polished off my pillow,
my blanket, and my sheet.
My homework seems to be the
only thing he will not eat.

Dear Santa, Did You Get My Tweet?

Dear Santa, did you get my tweet
of presents I would think are
sweet?
And what about my Facebook post
of toys and stuff I want the most?

Dear Santa, did you read my blog?
That's where I keep a running log
of all the times that I've been
good
and doing things I know I should.

I hope you saw my Instagram,
my email wasn't flagged as spam,
you've seen my YouTube channel
too,
and all my texts have made it
through.
Wait, does the North Pole even get
computers and the Internet?
I hope it does. I mean, it better,
or I might have to write a letter.

I Tried to Do My Homework

I tried to do my homework
but a show was on TV.
A song was on the radio.
A friend was texting me.

My email chimed, and so, of
course,

I had to look at that.
It linked me to a video
of someone's silly cat.

I watched a dozen videos,
and then I played a game.
I almost didn't hear her
when my mother called my name.

I looked up at the clock
and it was time to go to bed.
I didn't get my homework done;
just other stuff instead.

I hope my teacher listens
to the cause of my inaction.
It's really not my fault the world
is just one big distraction.

Random Miranda

I'm Random Miranda.
Bananas are good.
Remember the alphabet.
Elephants would.

The things that I tell you,
may seem rather strange,
but that's just because
here's a dollar in change.

And next week I'm going to
isn't this fun?
So never let anyone
hamburger bun.

If maybe you're wondering
what's going on,
please let me explain it:
The milk is all gone.

When doing your homework,
that man is a spy.
I'm happy to see you.
Just give it a try.

This pencil is purple

and everyone should.
Your dad is a doughnut.
Bananas are good.

This may seem bizarre but
it's just what I do.
I'm Random Miranda,
so thanks for the shoe.

My Very Long Poem

My

teacher

said

to

write

a

p
o
e
m

a
n
d

m
a
k
e

i
t

n
i
c
e

a
n
d

l
o
n

g

.

I

d

i

d

e

x

a

c

t

l

y

w

h

a

t

s

h

e

a

s

k

e
d
.

S
o

w
h
a
t

d
i
d

I

d
o

w
r
o
n
g
?

Candy Love

Chocolate assortments
and little pink hearts.
Hershey's Kiss Roses
and sour SweeTarts.

All of these candies
arrived with some cards,
sending me mushy
romantic regards.

Valentine's Day,
what a troublesome date.
Don't like the cards,

but the candy is great!

I Tried to Ride a Skateboard

I tried to ride a skateboard.
I fell and scraped my knee.
I tried to ride a bicycle.
I crashed into a tree.

I tried to ride a scooter.
I landed on my chin.
I tried to ride a unicycle;

lost a bit of skin.

I even tried a tricycle
but ran into a wall.
I'm happy in this wheelchair now.
I never fall at all.

My Smartphone Isn't Very Smart

My smartphone isn't very smart.
In fact, it's rather dumb.
It's dumber than a doorknob
or a piece of chewing gum.

It used to be so awesome,
but now my phone is lame.
It cannot surf the Internet.
It cannot play a game.

It can't take any pictures.
It can't install an app.
It won't look up my email
or an address on a map.

It won't play any music.
It cannot calculate.
It won't bring up a calendar
to show the time or date.

It cannot send a message.
It cannot make a call.
It's safe to say my smartphone
won't do anything at all.

It wasn't always like this.
Perhaps you'll take a peek?
I don't know why it acts this way.
I charged it just last week!

Bigfoot's Bewilderment

My head is humongous.
My neck is tremendous.
My legs are so long that
my stride is stupendous.

My chest is impressive.
My torso's titanic.
My arms are enormous.
My hands are gigantic.

My thighs are the size
of a couple of boulders.
I'm thick in the hips and
immense in the shoulders.

I'm broad as a tree trunk.
I'm tall as a tower.
My epic proportions
could cause you to cower.

I'm big in the belly.
I'm wide in the seat.
I'm really unclear why
I'm known for my feet.

Don't Think About a Zebra

Don't think about a zebra
no matter what you do,
for, if you ever think of one,
then, soon, you'll think of two.

And, after that, you'll think of
three,
and then you'll think of four.
Then five or six or seven zebras;
maybe even more.

And then you'll think of zebra
herds
stampeding down the street,
and zebras wearing tutus,
disco-dancing to a beat.

You'll think of flying ninja zebras
practicing kung fu.
And zebra clowns from outer space.
And robot zebras too.

And zebras in pajama bottoms
bouncing on their beds,

and maybe even zebras
wearing diapers on their heads.

You'll wish you'd never thought of
them,
so do it starting now:
Don't think about a zebra.
Only think about a cow.

My Cow Bess

I'd like to introduce you to my
cow.
Her name is Bess.
She has a special talent that
I know you'd never guess.

She's fond of eating chocolate
which I feed her every day.
The chocolate makes her happy so
she starts to swing and sway.

She jiggles and she joggles.
She wiggles and she whirls.

She boogies and she bounces.
She taps and twists and twirls.

She shivers and she shudders.
She quivers and she quakes.
I feed her chocolate candy and
she gives me chocolate shakes.

My Baby Brother's Birthday

My baby brother's birthday
was a fabulous affair.
The birthday cake was in his lap,
the frosting in his hair.

He threw the ice cream at the
walls;
it splattered on the rug.

And then he dumped his apple juice
in mommy's coffee mug.

He tore the wrapping paper off
of all his brand new toys,
then pounded them to see which ones
would make the loudest noise.

We've never had a party that
was such fantastic fun.
I guess they're simply better
when your brother's turning one.

Nobody Touch My Tarantula Sandwich

Nobody touch my tarantula
sandwich.
This sandwich is only for me.
And please stay away
from my cockroach soufflé
and my cobra and rat fricassee.

Don't take a swig of my
spider-blood cider,
or nibble my lizards on rye.
And don't make a meal
of my barbecued eel

or my rattlesnake-jellyfish pie.

Please keep your paws off my
octopus pudding.
Don't dine on my porcupine dip.
And don't have a chew
of my centipede stew
or a sip of my scorpion whip.

If I had Snickers, or Hershey's, or
Reese's,
I promise I'd offer to switch,
but there's no good eating
for kids trick-or-treating
outside of the home of a witch.

My Brother's a Bother

My brother's a bother.
My mother and father
say, "Don't bother him
and he won't bother you."

But bugging my brother,
one way or another,
is one of the things that
I most like to do.

I like to annoy him.
I really enjoy him
whenever he's yelling,
"You're being a pest!"

My father and mother
say, "Don't bug your brother!"
But bugging my brother
is what I do best.

It's really exciting
whenever we're fighting.
It's awesome to argue
and never agree.

But I'll have to quit it.
I hate to admit it,
but maybe the bothersome
brother is me.

I'm Lonely, So Lonely

I'm lonely, so lonely.
I'm always alone.
I never get emails
or calls on my phone.
I sit by myself
in my room every day,
and wonder why nobody
wants to go play.
My classmates avoid me.
They never say, "Hi."
They don't seem to know
I'm a wonderful guy.
And even the strangers
I see on the street
go out of their way
to make sure we don't meet.
They jump up and run
to get out of my path.
I guess maybe this year
I'll take my first bath.

My Favorite Food Is Broccoli

My favorite food is broccoli.
I eat it every day.
There isn't any other food
that makes me feel this way.

It makes me feel so healthy.
It makes me look so cute.
But, mostly, I like broccoli
because it makes me toot.

Instructions for Painting a Self-Portrait

1. Get yourself a mirror
and some brushes
and some paint.

2. Paint the mirror
where your face is.
Don't paint where it ain't.

My Mother Does My Homework

My mother does my homework.
She thinks it's loads of fun.
She says that she's just "helping"
me
but, soon enough, it's done.

We sit down at the dinner table
every single night.
She answers all the questions
and she always gets them right.

And, now and then, she'll tell me
I should go and take my bath.

When I get back, I find she's done
my science and my math.

You'd think that I'd be overjoyed
to never have to work.
But every time she "helps me out"
I nearly go berserk.

I ask if I can do it, but
she shrugs off my requests,
so all my grades are crummy
since she doesn't take my tests.

My Sister Says She's Sleepy

My sister says she's sleepy,
that her energy is sapped.
She says she'd feel much better
if she climbed in bed and napped.

She says she feels so drowsy
that she has to shut her eyes.
She just can't keep from closing them
no matter how she tries.

She's claims she's so exhausted
that she cannot stay awake.
She swears that she'll be useless
till she has a little break.

She says she needs to catch some
Z's,
to hit the hay, to doze,
to hibernate, to dream,
to have a moment of repose.

I'm pretty sure she's faking
when she jumps in bed and snores.
You see, this happens every time
our mom says, "Do your chores."

I Took My Doggy for a Walk

I took my doggy for a walk.
I thought it would be fun.
The moment that we got outside
he took off at a run.

I gripped the handle of his leash.
It instantly pulled tight.
My dog was strong. He ran so fast

I practically took flight.

He pulled me through the
neighborhood.
(My doggy likes to roam.)
I bumped and bounced and banged
around
until he ran back home.

So now I'm bruised and battered
like a ratty, tattered rag.
I took my doggy for a walk.
He took me for a drag.

Nate the Creative

I'm Nate the Creative
and here's what I do:
I wake up each day and
create something new.

I might bake a pickle
and skyscraper pie.
I might take a nickel
and teach it to fly.

I might paint a picture
of checkerboard cheese,
or fashion a statue
from typewriter keys.

Or dream up a dance
where you stand very still,
or buy all of France
with a nine-dollar bill.

So look all you want
but you won't ever see
a person on earth
as creative as me.

Tomorrow, I might make

a hat out of you.
I'm Nate the Creative.
It's just what I do.

Our Teacher's a Hippie

Our teacher's a hippie,
like from some old movie.
He likes to say "trippy,"
and "far out," and "groovy!"

He dresses in tie-dye
and bell-bottom pants.
He listens to hi-fi.
"The Twist" is his dance.

He says, "psychedelic!"
He's truly old-school.
He may be a relic,
but, boy, is he cool!

Dear Summer

Dear Summer, you're always my favorite.
I really do like you a lot.
You come every year,
and I'm glad when you're here.
I don't even mind that you're hot.

Dear Summer, whenever you visit,
I love to go outside to play.
I get to wear shorts
and play summertime sports,
or sometimes do nothing all day.

I put on my goggles and swim
suit,
and head for the beach or the
park.
I go for a hike
or I ride on my bike,
and stay awake long after dark.

Dear Summer, I'm glad you could
join us.
without you, it won't be the same.
I promise I know
that you do have to go,
but, still, it seems sort of a shame.

I'm sure that I'm going to miss
you.
The school year is finally here.
I had so much fun
playing out in the sun.
I guess that I'll see you next year.

ABOUT THE AUTHOR

Children's Poet Laureate (2013-2015) Kenn Nesbitt is the author of many books for children, including *The Armpit of Doom, More Bears!, The Tighty-Whitey Spider,* and *One Minute Till Bedtime.* He is also the creator of the world's most popular children's poetry website, www.poetry4kids.com.

More Books by Kenn Nesbitt

One Minute Till Bedtime – It's time for tuck-in, and your little one wants just one more moment with you–so fill it with something that will feed the imagination, fuel a love of reading, and send them off to sleep in a snap! Little Brown Books for Young Readers.

Bigfoot Is Missing – Children's Poets Laureate J. Patrick Lewis and Kenn Nesbitt team up to offer a smart, stealthy tour of the creatures of shadowy myth and fearsome legend. Bigfoot, the Mongolian Death Worm, and the Loch Ness Monster number among the many creatures lurking within these pages. Chronicle Books.

Believe it or Not, My Brother Has a Monster – From one scary monster to ten disgusting slugs and everything in between, this spooky story is full of creepy crawlies ... and one nervous little brother! Scholastic.

Kiss, Kiss Good Night – Snuggle up with this bedtime poem, all about how mommy animals say good night to their little ones. Cartwheel Books.

The Biggest Burp Ever – Seventy more poems about wacky animals, comical characters, funny families, silly situations, and much, much more.

The Armpit of Doom – Seventy new poems about crazy characters, funny families, peculiar pets, comical creatures, and much, much more.

The Ultimate Top Secret Guide to Taking Over the World – Are you fed up with people telling you what to do? You're in luck. Just read this book and in no time at all you will be laughing maniacally as the world cowers before you. Sourcebooks Jabberwocky.

MORE BEARS! – Kenn Nesbitt's picture book debut will have you laughing while shouting "More Bears!" along with the story's disruptive audience. Sourcebooks Jabberwocky.

The Tighty-Whitey Spider: And More Wacky Animals Poems I Totally Made Up – With poems like and "I Bought Our Cat a Jetpack" and "My Dog Plays Invisible Frisbee," this collection shines with rhymes that are full of jokes, thrills, and surprises. Sourcebooks Jabberwocky.

My Hippo Has the Hiccups: And Other Poems I Totally Made Up – *My Hippo Has the Hiccups* contains over one hundred of Kenn's best-loved poems. Sourcebooks Jabberwocky.

Revenge of the Lunch Ladies: The Hilarious Book of School Poetry – From principals skipping school to lunch ladies getting back at kids who complain about cafeteria food, school has never been so funny. Meadowbrook Press.

When the Teacher Isn't Looking: And Other Funny School Poems – *When the Teacher Isn't Looking* may be the funniest collection of poems about school ever written. This collection of poems by Kenn Nesbitt is sure to have you in stitches from start to finish. Meadowbrook Press.

The Aliens Have Landed at Our School! – No matter what planet you live on, this book is packed with far-out, funny, clever poems guaranteed to give you a galactic case of the giggles. Meadowbrook Press.

For more funny poems, visit www. poetry4kids.com

Back Cover Material

MY CAT KNOWS KARATE

Kenn Nesbitt returns with another round of the ridiculous rhymes, wacky wordplay, and preposterous punchlines that kids love to read.

My Cat Knows Karate includes seventy new poems about goofy gadgets, kooky characters, funny families, absurd situations, and much much more.

Be sure to visit Kenn online at the world's most popular poetry site for kids:
www.poetry4kids.com

www.ingramcontent.com/pod-product-compliance
Lightning Source LLC
Chambersburg PA
CBHW072156090426
42740CB00012B/2285